To

Nenita

Dear Single Lady

31 Practical Wisdom For Dating And Receiving Your Prophetic Marriage

Zofaa Publishing
Atlanta, Georgia

© 2018 Uyi Abraham
www.DearSingleLady.com

ISBN: 9781724133540

All rights reserved. Printed in the United States of America

Published by www.zofaapublishing.com

No part of this publication may be reproduced, sold, emailed or transmitted in any form without the prior permission of the author except in the case of brief quotations within critical articles and reviews.

Except otherwise quoted, scripture quotations are from the King James Version® © 1982 by Thomas Nelson, Inc. Used by permission. All rights reserved.
Amplified Bible (AMP) Copyright © 1954, 1958, 1962, 1964, 1965, 1987 by The Lockman Foundation. The ESV® Bible (The Holy Bible, English Standard Version®) is adapted from the Revised Standard Version of the Bible, copyright Division of Christian Education of the National Council of the Churches of Christ in the U.S.A. All rights reserved. Scripture quotations marked (MSG) are from *The Message* by Eugene H. Peterson. © 1993, 1994, 1995, 1996, 2000. NavPress Publishing Group. Scripture quotations marked (NLT) are from *Holy Bible*, New Living Translation. © 1996, 2004, 2007. Tyndale House Publishers, Inc. All rights reserved. Scripture quotations marked (CEV) are from Contemporary English Version ® Copyright © 1995 American Bible Society. All rights reserved.
(GW) GOD'S WORD® is a copyrighted work of God's Word to the Nations. Copyright 1995 by God's Word to the Nations. All rights reserved.
Holy Bible, New International Version®, NIV® Copyright © 1973, 1978, 1984, 2011 by Biblica, Inc.® Used by permission. All rights reserved worldwide.

Introduction

Single ladies have been neglected in the discourse of marriage. Most of the books and information out there blame them for being single. There aren't enough good practical teachings to help single women maneuver the complicated world of dating in the social media age and in choosing the right mate.

This stirred me up. How are women able to discern who is for them and who is not? How can they distinguish between when a guy is using them or genuinely interested? What are the red flags to look out for when viewing a potential mate that can lead to issues later on? The best part is that single women are getting answers from a man's perspective.

This is the cheat code for understanding a guy's mind on the matter of dating, courtship, and marriage.

I have been writing 'dear single lady posts' on social media for the past six years. For whatever reason, God has given me the grace to speak life to single women and encourage them in their place of singleness. I don't take this ministry lightly. Daily, I received numerous inboxes, emails, phone calls of women complaining about or expressing their dissatisfaction with their state of singleness.

Historically speaking, women have been neglected in their ability to create change in great things to happen and manifest in the earth. Yet there are many pressures on women that point them in the wrong direction, especially when it comes to marriage.

This book was written to help single ladies shift from 'single' to 'happily married!'

Don't read this book alone. Get a copy or copies for every single lady you know!

Happy reading!

Dr. Uyi Abraham
Love And Relationship Expert
www.DearSingleLady.com

Contents

1. Know who you are   9

2. Know what you want   13

3. Choose someone with character   17

4. Do your social media investigation   23

5. If he is not pursuing you, he is not into you   27

6. Take full advantage of the single season   31

7. The God factor   35

8. The first date tells everything   39

9. It's ok for you to be the first one to make the approach   41

10. If he is not spending money on you, he is not into you   45

11. You must be able to communicate freely   49

12. Deal with the soul issues   53

13. A confident woman is a sexy woman   57

14. Don't feel bad or apologize for wanting to be married   59

15. Don't invest in someone who cannot invest back into you   61

16. Ask the right questions   65

17. If you can't trust him now, you won't be able to trust him later   67

18. Break the soul tie before it breaks you   71

19. It is better to marry late to the right one than to marry early to the wrong one   75

20. You need an Eagle eye   77

21. Don't settle for a man who doesn't match your intellectual and spiritual levels   79

22. Identifying your baggage   83

23. Don't marry a guy who doesn't turn you on   87

24. Build your financial independence 91

25. Relationships shouldn't be just about sex 95

26. It is very dangerous to marry a narcissistic, self-centered and stingy man. Run! 97

27. Don't give up the Cookie (too soon) 101

28. 31 ways to know he's not into you 107

29. Demolishing spiritual forces of marital delays 111

30. Prayer to manifest your spouse 117

31. The two reasons why you are still single 121

Bonus: How to establish good credit 125

Dear Single Lady Coaching 133

1

Know Who You Are

Dear Single Lady, I want you to know that you are wonderful in the eyes of God. Actually, God said that you are fearfully and wonderfully made.

You are not an afterthought in the mind of God, so don't let your friends, family, or society make you act like one. Any successful dating and marriage relationship begins with you knowing who you are in Christ.

A lady who doesn't know who she is will suffer in the hands of uncaring men.

The expectations that you have of life are different when you recognize who you are and what God has in store for you. You may not be clear about every single thing God has for you; that's OK, but you should know enough to know the things that are most important to you. *It is hard for a man to really know how to please and serve you if you don't know what will please and serve you.* You should have enough understanding of yourself to communicate to him so that you can best be fulfilled. When you don't know, you have the greatest tendency to settle for what comes your way.

So, I want you to resolve within you your purpose, your calling, your assignment, and your identity.

Your purpose is found in the specific problems that God created you to solve. You were never made or expected by God to solve every problem or to be everything to everyone. You were created by God to be the solution to some precise problems. Everything that God made was with the intention to solve a problem and add value to the existing situation or environment. If you don't decode your purpose, you have robbed your generation of your blessing.

Discovering your purpose in life will help you greatly in choosing a mate. In my opinion, this is the foundation for dating and marriage. A lady who has discovered who she is will be ready to receive a man who would complement her.

Develop your capacity to be loved. You were coded for first-class living. I know that might sound cheesy, but it's so true. Royalty is inside of you. You were planned to live a wonderful, blessed, electrifying and productive life. Your purpose is not your personal undertaking; it's God's divine idea for your existence. Purpose can also be seen as the reason that God created you. God never wasted any creation. You were not born to merely exist but to live out a set divine plan.

Your purpose is the same as knowing your identity.

Find yourself so that someone else can find you.

When you know who you are, you will know who you are not. When you know who you are not, you'll also know how never to settle for any man again.

Discover your wonderful, divine identity and never settle again. You are worth waiting for. You deserve to be treated with the best chivalry and luxury the world has ever seen. So you need to work on yourself first before you make yourself available for dating or courtship. This is where so many people miss it. They're waiting for Mr. Right or Mrs. Right to show up instead of making themselves the right one first in anticipation for their future spouse.

Preparation time is never a wasted time. Invest in yourself. Know who you are!

Scripture Meditation: "For I know the plans I have for you, says the Lord. They are plans for good and not for evil, to give you a future and a hope" (Jeremiah 29:11, TLB).

2

Know What You Want

Society makes you feel like you have to wait like a sitting duck for someone to find you. No, you decide! You decide who and what you like in a potential mate. You are a daughter of God—The King! You're royalty, you have divine blood flowing through your veins, and you have a divine right to decide who you want to marry and spend the rest of your life with.

So, allow me to ask you the million-dollar question: What do you want in your mate?

If you don't know who and what you want, you will settle for anyone and anything that comes your way. Let me say it again, you have a right to decide who you want. Do you want a tall man for a husband, maybe six feet and five inches in height? Or are you only attracted to funny and easy-going men?

The truth is that there are plenty of men out there who might be great for other women but do not match your spiritual, intellectual, or mental levels. So be it! Wait for your own kind of man, and before you know it, he will be right there by your side.

Dear Single Lady, you'll have to know who you want; don't allow people to try to shove just any kind of man down your throat. Also, don't get desperate because of the so-called biological clock that you rush and receive just any man into your castle. You are a queen, and you deserve a king that is suitable for you.

Don't let others decide for you who you should marry. Find who you are so you can find the right person.

I encourage you to use a **top 10 list.** *Use the list to write out the top 10 qualities you desire in your mate.*

They can be physical characteristics or personality-based characteristics. You'll find you will have a much stronger relationship when the both of you share common values and attributes.

You don't have to be 100 percent compatible in order to make a long-term relationship work, but there are a few areas that you'll find it beneficial to have partner compatibility.

Your values and morals have to match. It is often said that opposites attract. It's mostly false in marriage and relationship-building. It is pointless to date or marry someone who is so fundamentally different from you in terms of values and morals. Like the Bible says, light and darkness cannot co-exist. A good example: If you believe strongly in monogamy, and the person you're dating believes in having numerous sexual partners, that would equal incompatibility.

For the both of you to have a loving and happy relationship together, your life dreams and core visions must align. You both need to have similar worldviews and goals in life. It doesn't need to be the same goals, dreams, and visions but not too far apart that you both can't see eye to eye the future destination of your relationship. If you want to be a lawyer, but he wants to be a drug dealer, then you both are not compatible!

The person you want to be with has to be one that stimulates you mentally and matches your intellectual curiosity and brain power. For example, a person with a Ph.D. dating a person with a 2nd-grade educational level; they might not have a lot they can converse about. They are both on two mental and intellectual spectrums.

You want to spend your life with someone that can make love to your mind as well as your body. You will know if someone is compatible with you. You will be able to speak to the person easily and have a good time being around him.

Here is an example of a top 10 list:

1. Christian
2. Physically Attractive
3. At least 6 feet tall
4. Financially stable
5. Family oriented
6. Wants children
7. Ambitious and a hard worker
8. Happy and positive minded
9. Strong leader and protector
10. College educated

Now, you go write your own top 10 list!

Scripture Meditation: "Can two walk together, unless they are agreed?" (Amos 3:3, NKJV).

3

Choose Someone With Character

She stormed into my office without an appointment, eyes blazing red, hair undone flowing in the wind. Her fist tightening with every step she took towards me. I'm in trouble. I could see the first punch before it landed on my face—though it didn't happen. *What's going on?* I wondered. I managed to scramble under my breath, "Hmmn … Hello, Janice; how are you?" No response!

I wrote this story in greater detail in my previous relationship book titled *No Time To Settle.*

I could already tell that this unscheduled meeting was going to be unusual. Something was wrong, and I wanted to find out what it was. I had known Janice for five years. I had been a mentor and spiritual counselor to her.

She had dated several men through the years, and her relationships always ended in ways that left her heartbroken and emotionally devastated.

Janice finally came to a halt less than three feet from my desk. "Dr. Abraham, I never imagined my life to be like this. I have done all I know to do—read many books, attending all the conferences recommended by my closest friends. I've invested in myself, gotten healthier in my character like you told me to, and yet I keep having the same experiences over and over again."

She continued, "Why am I still single? Why do I keep dating these dumb-ass men?"

"Excuse me, Janice; you can't curse in my office," I fired back.

"I am so sorry, Pastor; please forgive me," she said.

"You're forgiven! I think you need to control your emotions; have a seat and let's talk," I replied

She hurried to a seat and tried to compose herself, sobbing slightly.

"But why are my dating experiences horrible? Why can't I find a good man to love me and accept my children? Why am I not married yet?" she inquired, raising her voice just a little.

Janice's dating life had been horrible since she got divorced about ten years ago. As a single mother, it had been her desire to be married again, but the problem is that she keeps dating guys with little or no character.

She's not alone in this dilemma. There's a good chance that you reading this book have chosen someone for reasons other than **character.**

Dear Single Lady, character is the first rule of love and prophetic marriage. To have a fulfilling, exciting and blissful relationship, you must date a guy with proven character.

Janice was shocked because she didn't heed to my earlier counsel that any sustainable relationship must start by dating someone who has character.

Character is the first rule of dating. You see, dating and marriage are not as complicated as most people seem to believe. They both can be heavenly and blissful. Everything that functions in life has established principles that govern it, likewise dating and marriage. Character is the first rule of dating. If you ignore the first rule, the other rules will not work.

What Janice wanted was a man to love her unconditionally and be committed to her in a dating relationship leading to marriage.

Character doesn't mean a guy has to be perfect. No! It means they have to have certain strong attributes and values that align with yours. It means they are upright and have depth within their soul. Their soul is strong with moral and spiritual standards. *A guy without character is totally unpredictable; they won't care about you or your feelings when it counts the most.*

They make decisions moved by their own personal feelings, situations, circumstances, greed, or self-interests over general interest. Have you been through this? He's charming, fun and sexy, and he wants you! He pursues you, asks you out and lavishes you with attention. He knows all your emotional 'hot buttons' right up front and pushes them freely. You begin falling in love, hoping that he's 'the one.' There's just one little problem—his character.

You might be so attracted to him or her, but do they have the character to commit to a long-term relationship with you?

How to know if he has character?

Here is what I found out – If he cannot commit to a job, he can't commit to one woman. Job history can also show us something about a person's character.

Watch his behavior. His behavior will show you if he has character or not. Do you see signs of instability in his life? How does he treat other people? How many ladies has he dated in the last two years? How did his last relationship end? How long ago was that?

What about his temper? *A dishonest person can never be faithful to you in a relationship.*

A guy that's high on charisma but low on character is a disaster waiting to happen. It's important that you know that. Looks can be deceptive. Don't get into the dating phase too quickly until you have spent sufficient time with someone, and you can attest to their character as that which is compatible with yours.

All might fail, but character will endure till the end. Understand this: when you build your own character, you will start to attract men of character into your life.

I can't tell you enough how many times I have seen single ladies make this major mistake and pay a huge price for it.

Scripture Meditation: "A good name is more desirable than great wealth. Respect is better than silver or gold" (Proverbs 22:1, GW).

4

Do Your Social Media Investigation

As a sex and relationship expert, I never imagined I'd spend so much time talking to single ladies about the good and perils of Instagram, Facebook, Twitter, and Snapchat. It's no secret that our relationships are forming over apps and swipes.

You don't need to blind-date anymore; you can know more about a person even before they ask you out!

As a single woman, know that social media will reveal more to you about a relationship interest than they could ever tell you about themselves.

Social media tells a lot about a person. It helps to reveal who they are and the things that occupy their thoughts and attention. Don't neglect this opportunity for information gathering. Be sure to investigate your potential guy on social media. Follow them, like their account, have someone else like their account and see the things that they hit like button on. If your guy constantly likes pictures of scantily clad women, you have the right to ask some questions. Mature men may look, but they have enough discipline not to hit 'like.' Immature men look, like and comment because they lack the discipline or the self-growth needed to bypass things that tantalize their eyes.

Read his posts and the posts of his friends and the kind of people he follows on social media. Social media reveals a lot about people's character. Nowadays, you don't need to hire a private investigator to tell you about somebody; just follow them on social media.

Now, if you find some things on his social media accounts that trouble you, don't overlook it. *If you overlook it now, you will regret it tomorrow.*

Have the conversation. Without conversation, you can never know exactly what someone is thinking. When you have a standard of what is acceptable or not acceptable, you can determine if his answer will work for you. This is a skill that you will have to master for marriage. You have to be able to communicate things in a way that will allow you to gain insight and understanding while expressing yourself.

Here is another social media tip: if he is privately inboxing you and expressing his feelings to you but will not share those same feelings publicly on his social media pages, you already know that he is hiding something from you.

If his social media friends don't know you as his girl, then you are not official in his life!

It is very difficult for you to know a person without knowing the people they surround themselves with. If you have not met his friends or even some of his family members even on social media, that is a red flag. People who are important to you should meet the other people who are important to you. Without seeing those people, it will be difficult for you to know how well he treats others.

The way that they treat others is an indicator of how they will treat you. *Everyone knows that people put on their best behavior within the first 30 days of a new relationship.* But it's hard to bake a lie for an extended period of time. That is why it's good to date a while so you can get a clearer picture of the one who you may spend the rest of your life with.

I also want you to check their social media friends. If they don't have many friends, they treat their friends poorly or are hiding their friends from you, you'll need to begin to disengage. Your love interest's friends are also going to be a great resource to find out their habits with the opposite sex as well as how they behave in various situations in life.

Dear Single Lady, use social media to investigate your relationship interest without stalking them!

Scripture Meditation: "Lips that lie are disgusting to the LORD, but honest people are his delight" (Proverbs 12:22, GW).

5

If He Is Not Pursuing You, He Is Not Into You

When a man truly wants you, he has NO excuse. He pursues you until he wins your heart and PUTS a ring on your finger!

There is literally no excuse for a man who truly loves you or has deep emotions for you. There are people who do not live in the same city, the same country, yet they find a way to express their love and admiration for the woman they proclaim to love.

When a man is constantly thinking about you, he will consider ways to make you think about him as well. **Men are equipped and built to chase, to pursue.** When you do not see that, or it is lackluster and full of excuses, then you must take that as a sign to excuse yourself from him.

Depending on the type of man you are dealing with, many of them will go along with the 'relationship' unless or until you put your foot down and demand commitment. You don't have to wait to have the conversation or express yourself clearly and firmly. If he does not reciprocate or change behavior, there are many others who will.

Dear Single Lady, *you deserve to have a guy who is madly in love with you and wants to make you his queen.*

Do not allow yourself to fall in love with someone who doesn't feel that way about you! This is one of the hardest things to accept when it comes to love and happiness.

You're special and awesome in God's eyes. Don't settle for less than you really deserve from God. You got no time to settle. *Your heart and love is precious; don't give it out to an unworthy person.*

Maybe you met a guy recently, and you're head over heels, but they don't seem keen. You're desperately going over and beyond just to make him realize how much you love him, but he is just as cold as the freezer in his response to you.

Sooner or later, he will tell you that things aren't working out, and he wants to move on, but you don't want to hear it. You try to persuade him to stay. Maybe you try to change, to become the person he really wants, but things are still the same. It never works because there are some people that will never love you, no matter what you do for them. The more you try to convince him to stay or to love you, the more you're damaging your self-esteem, self-worth, and destiny!

Don't beg anyone to love you or pursue you! If the only time he shows you any kind of affection is when he wants sex from you, money, or when you have to jump through the hoops, then you know he doesn't love you. *You see, no matter how much you love him, if he doesn't love you back, the relationship will never work.* If you have to beg, plead, cry, or manipulate anyone to love you, you'll have to do the same to try to make them stay.

God has created someone for you to love you unconditionally. You need and deserve someone who loves you for who you are. Don't settle for less.

As soon as you discover that you're with someone who really doesn't love you, you'll need to be brave and end the relationship before they do! You might feel bad for ending the relationship, but in due time, you will be so glad that you did.

A selfish and immature person will be a terrible dating partner and even worse as a spouse.

Dear Single Lady, stop buying the excuses of why he can't or won't pursue you. Enough of his excuses and sad tales on why he is not pursuing you. If a guy truly wants you, he will chase and pursue you and scale mountains, leap over buildings, swim through the oceans just to have you.

Let me tell you the truth.com on this: If you chase the man into the relationship, you will have to chase him to the altar. **If you have to chase him to the altar, you will have to chase him throughout your marriage.** And if you have to chase him throughout your marriage, you will get tired and end up despising your situation.

Scripture Meditation: "He who finds a wife finds a good thing, And obtains favor from the Lord" (Proverb 18:22, NKJV).

6

Take Full Advantage Of The Single Season

Maximize your single reason to its fullest advantage! Get yourself ready for you king.

Singleness is not a curse. Don't let people make you feel like you are cursed just because you're still single. Take advantage of your single season by learning more about yourself and receive healing from the pains of the past.

Travel and expose yourself to different cultures and food; do things that are exciting to you and will help you have an identity even when you get married.

Your time of singleness is one of the best times to identify yourself outside of the various roles that you would take in the future. Before you identify yourself as a wife, before you identify yourself as a mother, you must have an idea about yourself.

No secure man is going to want to have someone who doesn't have a clue as to who she is outside of him or the other roles that she will take on.

This is the time for you to get that degree, work on your credit, lose the weight, get rid of that emotional baggage in preparation of your prophetic marriage.

Waiting is not wasting. Don't receive that lie of the enemy. Just because you are single does not mean that you are wasting away. I understand that many women have been waiting for many years to find the love of their life, remarry, etc., but know this: you are single for a **reason** and a **season**.

Singleness does not last always unless you decide that you want it to last.

When you make a decision that you will be married, and you are operating in faith, you'll begin to speak it out, live it out and work it out.

Your faith will produce actions that will now stir you and your faith up, which will cause the heavens to bring forth the spouse you desire. Never forget, God gives us the desires of our heart when our desires line up with Him.

Don't wait for someone to take you out; take yourself out.

Your time of singleness is the time to enjoy yourself, your presence and, of course, God's presence. Don't wait for anyone to do anything for you. If you want to go out to eat, take yourself out to eat. If you want to go shopping, take yourself shopping.

This is the constant battle of being a single person. You can do things for yourself without waiting for someone else to do it for you.

Yet when your guy comes to do it for you, be ready to receive that blessing and gift. Leaving your life in the hands of others is a dangerous place to be in. Leave your life in the hands of God.

One of the most difficult things to do is to let go of the baggage we carry. We carried them for so long that they've now become a part of us.

I've seen single ladies claim a piece of baggage and make it their identity.

One single lady said to me the other day, "I am just an angry woman. That's who I am, and I've been this way since birth."

But the truth is, no one was born angry. Anger is not a fruit of the Holy Spirit. Anger is a spirit, and it's of the devil. A Christian should never have the spirit of anger in them. Also, know that some spirits such as anger can be inherited and passed on from generation to generation.

Look your best. Smell good at all times. Dress good and be sexy!

Scripture Meditation: "Before each young woman was taken to the king's bed, she was given the prescribed twelve months of beauty treatments—six months with oil of myrrh, followed by six months with special perfumes and ointments" (Esther 2:12, NLT).

7
The God Factor

A prophetic marriage starts with God. Putting God first in your relationship is the wisest investment you can ever make in your marriage.

A godless marriage is a marriage from hell.

Whether you are a spiritual person or not, God is the foundation of every marriage. He is the foundation because He created it. Because He created marriage, He alone can teach you how to have a marriage from heaven.

Every successful, satisfying relationship starts with a satisfying relationship with Jesus. As you develop that growing relationship with Jesus, He will fill up your love tank until it overflows. It will be easier for you to love and be loved. Seeking the face of God will cause a great spiritual growth in you that will have a positive effect on your marriage.

Like I said earlier, a growing relationship with Jesus is a must if you're seeking a blessed relationship and marriage. During tough times, you'll need something stronger than yourself to rely on to remain committed.

Loving God and having a strong and growing relationship with Jesus is not a requirement for you only but also for your mate. If a person cannot love God, how will they love you?

For God is love.

A good disciple of Jesus makes a good spouse. According to God, marriage is based on covenant. Covenant is not the type of relationship that you go back-and-forth from but rather the type that lasts for a lifetime.

By acknowledging God within your relationship, you acknowledge His standards, His ways, and His ideals in the treatment of each other. God's words provide a compass that both parties have to abide by and don't have the power to change.

A strong marriage has God in the midst of it. Experiencing the love of God teaches you what godly love looks and feels like. Also, a fulfilling relationship with Christ takes pressure away from your mate. You won't look for him or her to make you whole because you'll feel complete in Christ.

God desires that every couple live under His blessing and have successful and pleasurable lives. This happens to the extent that couples give and receive grace and truth in their relationship.

When you have God in your relationship, you and your spouse become a three-strand cord that cannot be easily broken. That is because you have now entered into a covenant with God and your spouse.

When I was single, this was number one on my compatibility test. I knew I was called to spend the rest of my life in ministry serving Jesus and helping people. It was crucial that I only date and eventually marry someone who had similar dreams and goals. Now, if I had dated and married a woman with a secular dream, you already see that even though her life dreams might be noble, we would not be compatible. Dating someone of a different religious background, differences in passion for God, or a different faith (example, a Christian dating a Muslim or an agnostic or an atheist) is not compatible and will not work.

I have to say, before you begin a dating relationship, put Jesus first. Every successful, satisfying relationship starts with a satisfying relationship with Jesus. As you develop that growing relationship with Jesus, He will fill up your love tank until it overflows. It will be easier for you to love and be loved. Seeking the face of God to make sure that this person you're considering is in God's plan for your life, consulting Jesus first even before you commit to the dating phase will help to save your time and energy from dating people in which the relationship is not going anywhere.

I've seen so many single and divorced people who went into a dating and marriage covenant with people who were the wrong one for them because they didn't seek the face of God. Don't go into dating someone or marrying someone without God's approval and blessings. God has someone special and custom-made just for you. God doesn't do near matches. His matches are divinely construed and perfect.

Scripture Meditation: "But seek first his kingdom and his righteousness, and all these things will be given to you as well" (Matthew 6:33, NIV).

8

The First Date Tells Everything

Dear Single Lady, a guy's true heart, character, and intention are revealed on the first date. One interesting fact about guys is that guys don't hide their feelings, mind, and emotions very well.

If on the first date, most of the conversation is gearing towards the color of your underwear, your favorite sex position, and sexual innuendos, you already know where his heart is. He is only looking for sex with you and nothing more.

A serious guy that is interested in a long-lasting relationship with you will NEVER bring up or stay long in sexual conversations on your first date.

Also, pay attention to the way he treats the waiter when the food arrives on the table late. Is he cool, calm and collected, or does he lose his temper?

On the first date, a guy that tipped well, let's say $20 or more to the server, is a generous guy. And generosity is a good factor for a guy to possess. A guy who was generous to the server or waiter will be kind and generous to you.

A guy who arrives late on the first date with no good alibi or excuse probably has no respect for you.

Don't waste your time with someone who doesn't value you or your time.

Listen and watch for clues on the first date. The first date often reveals a lot about a person than we often pay attention to.

Scripture Meditation: "For as he thinks in his heart, so is he. "Eat and drink!" he says to you, But his heart is not with you" (Proverbs 23: 7, NKJV).

9
It's OK For You To Be The First One To Make The Approach

I know this one may sound confusing or uncomfortable for you. I have seen so many happy and successful marriages over the years that resulted from the lady making the first approach. Hear me out, I have said this before and will continue to say it, women are not meant to pursue men. *Men should pursue, and women may approach.* Now do not misinterpret what I am saying.

A single lady may say 'hi' or pass your phone number to someone you are interested in. But ultimately, that man should pursue you if he is interested in you. He should want to spend time with you, get to know you, call you and find out about you as much as he can. Only players act like they don't care or don't want to chase after you.

John and Mary (not their real names) are good friends of mine. They have been together and married for many years with beautiful children among them.

They both attended the same church where Erica first saw Will and thought within herself that "he was cute." She decided to approach and make herself known to him. She left a note on his car one Sunday after church and pretty much let him know that she was interested in getting to know him better and available.

She didn't hear back from him in a couple of weeks. Their parts crossed again another time, and she mentioned to him that she did leave a note for him on his car, and she didn't hear back from him. They exchanged numbers, and the rest is history. In this radical prophetic marriage testimony, she made the first approach. She wasn't desperate for him or a man; she felt a strong inner witness to approach.

This kind of scenario may not work for everyone and may not be the way God chooses to bring your spouse to you. But I want you to be open minded and don't be dogmatic about traditional dating where the man always approaches the woman. The space in this book will not be enough for me to tell several other testimonies of many prophetic marriages that have happened because the woman approached first.

Some guys may be shy or easily intimidated by you or your success, and making the first approach may be that icebreaker he needs to give him the courage to pursue.

There is another story of a mentee of mine named Shirley, who was so blessed by one of the posts a man of God made on Facebook, and she inboxed him to let him know she was truly inspired, and if he felt the same, she would like for them to grab a coffee at some point since they were both in the same city.

To her surprise, he responded and said yes, he would love to know her better as well. One coffee date turned into another.

Eventually, they both realized that they were a match for each other. They have been married four years at the time of this writing.

Dear Single Lady, making the first approach doesn't mean you should stalk a man. It is not being thirsty and desperate for his attention.

Making the first approach can be as simple and innocent as being the first to say 'hello,' request for a date, lunch, public outing, etc.

It doesn't cheapen you to be polite or friendly to a guy that seems to fit your top 10 list.

Scripture Meditation: "Using a dull ax requires great strength, so sharpen the blade. That's the value of wisdom; it helps you succeed" (Ecclesiastes 10:10, NLT).

10

If He Is Not Spending Money On You, He Is Not Into You

I heard one FBI agent say, "If you are looking for a fugitive, follow the money." The direction of the flow of money will always lead to the fugitive. It's the same with love and dating. If he is not investing money on you, it's because he is not into you.

Most single ladies do not know that men look at a woman as an investment. If he's really into you, he will spend his money on you. He will take you out on dates and pay, shop for you, periodically put money in your hands and sometimes volunteer to help you with a bill—for example, your cell phone payment.

Now, if he is working but not spending money on you and keeps giving excuses for it, *I bet you 9 out* of 10 he is spending some kind of money on another woman rather than on you.

Here is another story from my book, *No Time To Settle*:

Temika was in love when she dated Jerome for three years and now married for another four years. Their marriage was rocky, and she met with me for a counseling session to try to save it. After a few questions, it became clear Jerome hasn't paid a single bill since they had been together. He had worked the whole time but would come up with excuses why he can't or shouldn't pay any bill in the house. She said she thought he was saving his money for their future together, only to realize that he had been spending his money on strippers, drinking, and taking exotic trips with other females.

Had Temika knew of this book, *Dear Single Lady*, she would have saved herself the headache and embarrassment of being with him. I wish I could tell you of a happy ending to this story, but unfortunately, they broke up and divorced. The truth is that Jerome really didn't care about her; if he did, he would have cared enough to contribute financially to their home and future.

Hear me, ladies; please don't be so blinded by 'love' or lust that you miss common sense clues about him.

Don't get so desperate for a man that you settle for just anything. God has not forgotten you. He is working on something and someone better. Dating you is not merely doing dinners, movies, ice creams, or hanging out. It's in really getting to know you, your dreams and heart desires, your pain and all that matters to you. Have him open the door for you and other chivalry expressions.

Money issues are one of the top three reasons that most relationships and marriages fail. One relationship expert says that money talk before marriage is the most important conversation to have before you say "I do."

The reality, however, is that if this relationship does go to the next level, you will be making money decisions together. Finding out if you are compatible when it comes to how you handle your daily money decisions could be a deal maker or a deal breaker.

According to a recent survey, 42% of couples do not talk about money before they are married. Bad money habits will cripple and burn out the love and sparks in a relationship faster than anything you can think about.

It's a plus for you both to educate yourselves about money. Discover and reveal your Money Personalities.

Talk about money. Money issues can make or break any relationship. Get healed and delivered from money issues before you say "I do."

Scripture Meditation: "For where your treasure is, there will be also your heart" (Matthew 6:21).

11

You Must Be Able To Communicate Freely

It is absolutely pointless to date or marry someone you can't freely communicate with.

Statistics show that communication is the number one reason why relationships and marriages fail. Open, honest communication should be part of every healthy relationship.

Dating is a time to talk and get to know each other. It is beyond a mere going out, hanging out and having a good time.

Don't date some who talks down to you, calls you names or berates you. You deserve better than that. If he has nothing to hide, he should be able to freely communicate and answer all of your questions.

God gave us mouth and ear so we can communicate with each other.

Good communication is one of the secrets of a strong marriage. Many marriages could be saved if spouses improved the ways they communicate with each other. It's often the simplest bad habits that get couples into trouble. Once a marriage gets on a rough track, negativity grows.

Defining expectations means you talk about everything that matters to you before the relationship gets deeper.

Share how many children you would like to have, where you would like to retire. Do you like to have a dog in the house or a cat? Would you like flowers every week?
Take the time to talk to each other. Tell him what you like and don't like.

Good communication deflects conflicts.

You cannot have a healthy marriage without good communication. Many broken marriages lie in the wake of good people invested in winning the argument who lose sight of their love for each other.

Conflicts arise in the relationship when we don't communicate well. Learn to listen to each other, not only to hear but to understand that they are trying to say to you. Learn how your spouse likes to hear and communicate that way to them.

I've seen many couples settle miserably because they didn't communicate before they started dating or get married. They talked about everything except themselves and their relationship.

The communication phase of dating is the discovery season where you should ask lots and lots of questions and don't take half-hazard answers. Ask at least 150 questions, including spirituality, politics, health, sex, sexual fantasies, children, in-laws, dreams, goals, ambitions, careers, strengths, and weaknesses.

Ladies, please know that men are not mind readers. If you can't tell us what is on your mind, we might never know. Tell us how to love you. Teach us how to love, honor and cherish you.

Sometimes ladies get frustrated when they asked him to pick up pancake mix from the store, and he came home with waffles mix. Men truly have basic hearing problems, and that is why you'll have to tell a man over and over again what you need without nagging him.

One of the reasons many do not communicate properly before jumping into relationships is that they don't know how to properly communicate.

One of a lady's most important needs is communication. Communication is as important to a lady as sex is to a guy. Sadly, most guys don't realize this until they are taught. Patient and loving communication connects a lady to her world.

Scripture Meditation: "Let your speech be always with grace, seasoned with salt, that ye may know how ye ought to answer every man" (Colossians 4:6, KJV).

12

Deal With Inner Healing And Soul Issues

When your soul is fragmented, it impairs your ability to flourish and grow as God had intended. A fragmented soul makes you make the wrong choices in men and relationships. It also makes the wrong kind of men who feed into your dysfunction and hurt find you.

With soul issues, your divine purpose in life is hindered, and the God kind of life set for you is suspended. Instead of experiencing life in its fullness, you experience life in hurt, pain, disappointment, frustration, and the like.

Now that we know better, no longer will we live a life that is fragmented because our souls are fragmented, but we will live a life that is whole because our soul is whole in Christ.

People + Trauma = SOUL ISSUES

Trauma is defined as a deeply distressing or disturbing experience. Furthermore, trauma comprises events or circumstances that took place which were improper for your age or against your will.

When these TRAUMATIC events occur and are left unresolved or unprocessed, they lead to the fragmentation of the soul—also referred to as the brokenness of the soul.

Past broken relationships, hurts, and pain can lead to soul trauma and mental dysfunction. When traumatic events continue to happen to an individual, it results in compounded trauma, and if the experiences and events are left unresolved, the soul takes on various fractions that have the ability to do a number of things to a person:

- pervert and manipulate your personality
- dismantle and destroy the way you perceive life and people
- destroy the way you perceive yourself
- fragment your ability to relate well with others
- distort your ability to make sound decisions

It also affects your emotions negatively, causing you to cultivate:

- bitterness
- rage
- anger
- resentfulness
- unforgiveness

... and other negative emotions that develop within the heart and soul due to traumatic events.

The way to reverse traumatic events is to properly and thoroughly process through them.

Processing through trauma allows the pain of the event to be stripped down into remnants. Those remnants can be used by God. But when traumatic events are left unprocessed, they become monuments [of pain] for the enemy to use.

The effects of trauma which create brokenness and/or fragmentation of the soul lead to:
- Soul issues
- Arrested development—mental, emotional, psychological, financial, sexual, spiritual
- Defense/coping mechanisms
- Cycles of dysfunction
- Self-sabotaging behavior

Some examples of trauma include:

- domestic abuse
- violence
- physical assault
- sexual assault
- divorce
- intense nightmares
- relocating and/or moving
- death of a close family member or loved one
- infidelity
- abandonment
- rejection from loved ones or people of importance to you
- car accidents
- life-jeopardizing acts of nature (floods, typhoons, earthquakes, etc.)
- loss of a child
- war
- incarceration
- abuse
- rejection or abandonment by parents

Scripture Meditation: "Beloved, I pray that you may prosper in all things and be in health, just as your soul prospers" (3 John 2).

13

A Confident Woman Is A Sexy Woman

A woman confident in her own skin is very attractive and sexy to a man. Confidence is very sexy because it shows a degree of independence and self-awareness. Confidence also draws people to you, especially men—because men like to be with a *promise* and not a *project*. Understanding how men think is paramount.

A real man wants a woman who will add to him and not be a deficit to him. A woman who adds to a man knows who she is, and she is confident in who she is. She has the ability to bring ideas, wisdom, connections, and other things that will help to make the man's life easier.

Tyler Perry produced a movie called "I can do bad all by myself." That is how men think as well. They can do bad all by themselves, but having a good confident woman will cause them to up level.

The Bible says it this way, "He who finds a wife finds a good thing and obtains favor." So, a woman will cause the favor of God to locate a man, and the favor of God will cause the man to be lifted up. Although some men cannot articulate this, this is automatically deposited in a man's DNA when he looks for a wife.

Many ladies erroneously think that physical beauty is what most attracts a guy to them. I want to tell you right now, a real man finds a confident woman very sexy and attractive.

So, you must be the kind of lady who is confident or at least appears to be able to bring something good to the life of that man.

Scripture Meditation: "Being confident of this, that he who began a good work in you will carry it on to completion until the day of Christ Jesus" (Philippians 1:6, NIV).

14

Don't Feel Bad Or Apologize For Wanting To Be Married

Dear Single Lady, your desire to be married is holy, and I pray that God will grant you your own spouse this year.

I have observed that society puts a lot of pressure on women to get married, have kids and establish a home by a certain age, yet if this is not done, they are chastised by that same society for desiring it. What's up with that!

Let's be clear, you are not your marital status.

You are a child of God. Whether or not you are married has no bearing on who God calls you to be. You can be marriage material but not married yet. You can be the type of wife any man would be excited to have but not married yet. This is why using the scripture to create a firm foundation within your heart is so important. Society will lead you astray.

People get married just for the sake of having a big wedding and putting the wedding pictures on Facebook and Instagram, but when they get home, their fairytale wedding is nowhere to be found. That is not your portion.

Stand tall knowing that what God has for you is for you. No devil in hell can stop it, no curse can bind it up forever, not even you can stop the goodness of God from finding you and bringing you your spouse! Don't allow outside pressure or the church to shake what should be happening on the inside.

God will grant you the desires of your heart regarding marriage. Don't feel bad or make excuses for wanting to be married.

Scripture Meditation: "Marriage is honorable in all, and the bed undefiled: but whoremongers and adulterers God will judge" (Hebrews 13:4, KJV).

15

Don't Invest In Someone Who Cannot Invest Back Into You

What's the point of being with someone if they can't teach you anything or add any value to your life? Most people like to look for a partner who complements their life instead of one who improves it.

I've found that if someone doesn't bring something to the table in a way that challenges how I think and act, or teaches me a thing or two about myself, the relationship becomes unproductive and regressive.

A healthy dating relationship adds value to its partners. Do not date someone who is not making contributions in your life. If he or she is not adding value to your life, they are worthless in your life. Contribution is about the person you're dating adding gain and value to you. That means he is investing in you and making your life better in every other way.

I've seen many wonderful single ladies investing too soon in an unproven relationship.

Let him lead in investing first in you.

Can he make you better in any way? That should be a foremost question in your mind as you contemplate a dating relationship. Ideally, you should grow together.

When you're deciding whether to stay in a relationship or not, ask yourself this question, *What has my time with this person taught me? Can he continue to contribute to my life and my goals?*

Some of you might think that this is a selfish way to think about it. But is it really selfish? I just think any serious relationship needs to add value to your life other than having someone to tell you "I love you" and who will always go to the movies with you.

Communication is one of the ways you can assess if someone can make a contribution or investment into your life or not. Ask them questions about how they can make a contribution to your life.

There is a difference between a temporal investment and a long-term investment. Sadly, many single ladies either date guys that are not investing in their lives at all or only making temporal contributions. Examples of temporal investments are: movie nights, phone calls, bringing you flowers, watching your kids while you go grocery shopping, etc.

You don't want to date someone who treats you like a casual partner and has no desire to be in a committed relationship. That's why you only need to date someone who loves and cares about you enough to put in the work required for your relationship to blossom.

Don't allow him into your heart too soon. See how he invests into you first.

It's hard for someone who you haven't allowed into your heart and soul to hurt you. Sometimes we open up our hearts too soon and get hurt too quickly, thereby ruining the chances of the relationship. Get to know someone well enough before you invite them into your heart. Your heart is a delicate thing to leave unprotected.

The point is that you're not going to find out if your new partner is selfish, a wife-beater, controlling, rude, immature, or unsympathetic in a few days. Take out time to discover if you both are compatible before you give them access into your heart.

You need time to honestly assess the relationship to see if you both are a match or not before you allow him into your heart. If you wait to commit, you might discover some things about that person that might not sit well with you. Know someone through all seasons before making any major decisions.

I have seen that falling in love too quickly often leads to falling out of love quickly as well. Guard your heart and emotions well.

Scripture Meditation: "Guard your heart more than anything else, because the source of your life flows from it" (Proverbs 4:23, KJV).

16

Ask The Right Questions

People can only pour into you what they have within them. Men are very much susceptible to this. The only thing that they have within them is what they can give to you. The way you can find out what is inside of a man is to ask the right questions. Find out what his family situation was.

Did he live in a single-parent home, parents who were married? Were the married parents functional or dysfunctional? Was a lot of love displayed? Did he get preferential treatment? Does he understand what it is to be a husband? What are his expectations of a wife?

There are many other questions to ask, but these questions help you to know what his capacity is as a man and a husband. If he did not have good examples when he was growing up, it will be very hard for him to figure out how to do or be a good example himself.

It is only when we are retrained or we intentionally expose ourselves to the right things that we have the ability to do those right things. Many women are looking for a man to display qualities that they have never seen before. Then they get upset when the man doesn't do it. This is the definition of insanity. I want you married, not insane.

The danger of marrying before you are mentally and emotionally ready is that you stand a higher chance of picking the wrong one.

Unfortunately, many ladies and people in general do this. I say unfortunately because it causes a myriad of problems that most people are unprepared to handle. Marriage is already messy as it is. *The last thing you want to do is bring in unnecessary baggage to add to the mix.*

Scripture Meditation: "With wisdom a house is built. With understanding it is established. With knowledge its rooms are filled with every kind of riches, both precious and pleasant" (Proverbs 24:3–4, KJV).

17

If You Can't Trust Him Now, You Won't Be Able To Trust Him Later

Dear Single Lady, if you can't trust 'em, don't date 'em. If you're having trust issues in a relationship, you may need to take a step back to examine why you have them and what you are going to do about it. Trust is essential in healthy relationships. If you don't have it, you really don't have a relationship.

Be realistic about what you see before marriage because that is a preview of what will happen after marriage.

I remember counseling Shalondria a few years back. She was a successful single mother with a good career ahead of her. She told me what was going on in her life and relationship. She'd been dating a guy for six years, and the relationship didn't seem to be going anywhere. She told me she just called off her engagement. I wondered why.

"Because I don't trust him," she said.

"I can't marry someone that I cannot trust," she concluded.

She went on to tell me so many stories of his lies. He told her when they first met that he had only two children, only for her to discover that he actually had four children from two previous marriages. She described so many other deceitful tendencies, unfaithfulness, and episodes of dishonesty.

You see, trust is one of the core foundations of any healthy relationship. When trust is missing, there's no relationship. It doesn't even matter how sexy, tall, dark and endowed he is. If you can't trust him, you'll never be happy. If you don't trust her, you will never feel safe, secure or happy with her.

Don't date someone who makes you feel insecure because you don't trust them. There are lots of reasons why you can't trust someone. Maybe they have a track record of being untrustworthy. Or maybe you just have hunches. Maybe they didn't tell the truth about some small things. Maybe he is innocent but just so secretive. Whatever it is, you'll need to have a talk with them.

There comes a point in every relationship when you get comfortable with your partner; you enjoy his company and don't see yourself without him. However, you still might find yourself second-guessing if you can really trust this guy.

It's just simple; there are people who are in it for the long haul, and then there are people who just want to get theirs and dip. It's important that you are able to distinguish between these categories, especially when you want to know if you can trust the person you are dating.

Here are the signs that you can't trust the guy you're dating:

1. He answers his phone in another room when he's around you.
2. His texts to you seem generic, and he doesn't use your name.
3. He doesn't have you as a friend on Snapchat or Facebook.
4. He's always working or unavailable at obscure hours.

5. He calls you by another girl's name more than once.
6. He is always with his ex.
7. He no longer cares for the things you care about.
8. He doesn't spend on you financially.
9. You are not included in his future plans.
10. He doesn't believe in monogamy.

When he's seen with other girls, he always says: "It's not what it looks like." There is no reason the man you're dating should be flirting or getting touchy with other girls. This is a huge no-go, and it shows that he has no respect for you. If you confront him, and he keeps saying, "It's not what it looks like," then you should know not to fall for this trap. Keep in mind it's exactly what it looks like.

So, if you don't trust your potential husband now, when you get married, those trust issues will deepen and get worse. Trust takes time to build and to develop. Yet it can take just a few seconds to destroy trust.

Scripture Meditation: "Some trust in chariots, and some in horses: but we will remember the name of the Lord our God" (Psalm 20:7, NJKV).

18

Break The Soul Tie Before It Breaks You

One of the reasons new relationships fail is that we're still stuck in the old ones and don't even know it. Soul ties are invisible bonds that wreak havoc in so many relationships and marriages.

A soul tie is an emotional bond or connection that unites you with someone else in your past or present. You can become bound to a person through your soul.

How to know you have a soul tie:

Have you found yourself tormented by thoughts about a person, excessively wondering about them, checking on them, rehearsing times with them? If so, you have soul ties. Have you grieved over a severed relationship with someone you were once close to? If so, you have soul ties.

Soul ties are formed through close friendships, through vows, commitments and promises, and through physical intimacy. Not all soul ties are bad. God wants us to have healthy relationships that build us up, provide wisdom and give godly counsel. God will strategically bring good relationships into our lives to form healthy soul ties just like in the case of David and Jonathan. See 1 Samuel 18:1 (AMP).

In contrast, Satan always brings counterfeits into our lives to form unhealthy soul ties.

A few ways unhealthy soul ties can be formed include:
• Abusive relationships (physically, sexually, emotionally, verbally)
• Adulterous affairs
• Sex before marriage
• Obsessive entanglements with a person (giving them more authority in your life than you give to God)
• Controlling relationships

Every time you have a sexual experience, you're creating deep-rooted bonds with the other person. This is one of the reasons why God says you should wait after marriage to have sexual relations with your partner.

Some symptoms of lingering soul ties include:

- Someone whose voice you hear in your head
- Obsessive day-time thought about someone
- Dreaming or waking up at night thinking about someone on a regular basis
- Still carrying the feelings of hurt caused by that person
- Reliving the moments of pleasure or pain with them

There are 4 Key steps to breaking soul ties:

1. Acknowledge
2. Confess and Repent
3. Forgive
4. Break and Remove

Pray this prayer aloud to help you break free from unhealthy soul ties: Lord God, I boldly approach Your throne of grace covered in the shed blood of Your Son. In Jesus' mighty name, I ask You to cut any and all ungodly soul ties between myself and anyone else created by any relationship, sexual or otherwise, known or unknown, remembered or forgotten. I decree, declare and prophesy that I am free from all new and past ungodly soul ties in Jesus' name. Amen!

You can also pray and break the covenant of ungodly soul ties by calling out the name of the person you need to be free from.

Pray like this: Lord God, In Jesus' name, I break and destroy any and all ungodly soul ties between myself and _____ (the person's name here). I free myself from that covenant, and I completely give my heart, soul, and body to You, Jesus! Amen!

Please note that until you break and untangle old unhealthy soul ties, you're not ready for a new healthy relationship. Do not carry past baggage into a new relationship.

Scripture Meditation: "Call on me in times of trouble. I will rescue you, and you will honor me" (Psalm 50: 15, GW).

19

It Is Better To Marry Late To The Right One Than To Marry Early To The Wrong One

I hope this statement brings you a sense of comfort, especially if you've been waiting for some time for your spouse. It really is better to wait to marry the right one than marry the wrong one early.

Many people can be in such a rush to enjoy marriage and forget or completely disregard that it comes with responsibility. A prophetic marriage requires both parties to bring their best self to the table in order to become one. But when you only have one person bringing their best self, it can cause a lot of friction and hurt.

There are many reasons why someone doesn't bring their best selves to the marriage such as immaturity, selfishness, emotionally unavailable, emotionally and mentally unprepared and no understanding of or examples of a healthy marriage.

My wife, Dr. Faith Abraham, is a counselor, and she can tell you countless stories of people who are or were married, yet suffered within their marriage because they didn't pay attention to the red flags or felt like when they got married, things would change.

Things don't change in marriage; things get magnified. I've seen many single ladies who decided to wait on God for the right one for them and were happily married after. God is on your side, and He has someone in mind just for you. As you pray for yourself, also pray for him that as he is being prepared for you, God will go in the areas of his emotions, mindset, and heart for you both to have the marriage intended by God.

Scripture Meditation: "For the vision is yet for an appointed time; But at the end it will speak, and it will not lie. Though it tarries, wait for it; Because it will surely come, It will not tarry" (Habakkuk 2:3, KJV).

20

You Need An Eagle Eye

Dear Single Lady, you need an eagle eye so you can see and smell every fake and counterfeit from 50 miles away.

The eagle bird has a unique vision and smell. It is among the strongest in the animal kingdom, with an eyesight estimated at 4 to 8 times stronger than that of the average human. An eagle is said to be able to spot a rabbit up to 50 miles away.

I pray that God gives you vision and sight like that of an eagle. I pray this prayer for you for many reasons. It is difficult for many women who are bombarded with societal pressure, the biological clock, feelings of loneliness, feelings of wanting to share their life with someone important, etc., to continue to have clear eyes to spot a counterfeit.

Think of it like $100 bill. It is not until you use that special yellow marker to mark the $100 bill that you can distinguish whether or not it is real. You need to have a yellow marker or, in other words, distinguishing factor(s) that will help you discern between the real godly man for you and a counterfeit.

Some of those factors can be:
• his treatment of other women, particularly his mom, sisters, and aunts
• his treatment of you; does he spend time with you, spend money on you? Did he introduce you to people who are important to him?
• his relationship history; does it contain red flags of anger, violence, neglect, or other things that are nonnegotiable for you?

Yes, people can change, yet people are also creatures of habit. So, pay attention to his habits or patterns of behavior.

Scripture Meditation: "But those who wait on the Lord shall renew their strength; They shall mount up with wings like eagles, They shall run and not be weary, They shall walk and not faint" (Isaiah 40:31, NKJV).

21

Don't Settle For A Man Who Doesn't Match Your Intellectual And Spiritual Levels

You are worth having someone that has the same capacity as you. Imagine yourself as a 20-ounce bottle of water. Your capacity is 20 ounces of water, but you settle for a 6-ounce bottle of water man.

This is a big problem because your capacity is greater than his capacity. Eventually, what you will try to pour into him, he will not be able to handle because he doesn't have enough capacity to deal with you and what you have to offer. How frustrating your life will be when you realize that your mate is unable to withstand you.

That is literally what it looks like to be unequally yoked. *You would rather have to wait for someone who has a similar if not greater capacity than you than be frustrated with someone who has a lower capacity than you.*

If a man cannot lead you to God, he is practically worthless in your life. Society makes you feel like you have to wait like a sitting duck for someone to find you. No, you decide! What do you want?

Decide for yourself what attributes, qualities, and characteristics of a man are important to you and what you believe is going to help your future. Your goal is not to build a man from scratch but rather an outline. For example, when you need to buy a new car, you begin to outline what kind of car you will get based on your requirements. If you need a vehicle that has good gas mileage, enough room for you and your kids and under $25k in price, wisdom will tell you to get a 4-door SUV. The car you choose will be based upon a variety of factors; likewise, the man that you choose will be based upon a variety of factors. You may not get every single thing on your list, but you will get enough to be happy and make a wise decision.

Marry a man who stimulates you spiritually and mentally. He has the mental and spiritual capacity to handle stimulating conversations with you.

I encourage you again to use a top 10 list. Use the list to write out the top 10 qualities you desire in your mate. They can be physical characteristics or personality-based characteristics. Either way, you have the opportunity to leave it up to others to decide, or you can decide.

When you meet different men or get approached by them, you have a standard of what is required.

Live your life before he comes. Be happy with you.

Live your life. Believe that your life is important and actually will add to the success of a marriage. This is why you have to be in tune with yourself. Your singleness is a time for you to become aware of your non-negotiable. What do you like? What don't you like? What are your values? What are the expectations that you have of your spouse? You have to be in tune with what you need in order to communicate that to your spouse. Otherwise, you will go along with whatever comes your way and will never be fulfilled within your marriage. This work begins before your marriage comes.

This time is great for reprogramming your soul. If you've never seen a healthy marriage, you can't expect yourself to be able to cultivate a healthy marriage.

Expose yourself to those who have it and learn the habits that cultivate a healthy marriage. If you're used to dysfunction, you have to take the time to repurpose your soul towards being healthy. It's only what is within you that you will be able to pour out.

Scripture Meditation: "I was glad when they said unto me, Let us go into the house of the Lord" (Psalm 122:1, KJV).

22

Identifying Your Baggage

I wrote in my bestselling book, *Marriage From Heaven,* about the importance of identifying and resolving any and all known baggage before you enter into a serious dating relationship or prophetic marriage.

Janet was only seventeen years old when she started dating Tyson. Their relationship was on and off for a few years. They later reconnected in college and married five years later. They picked up great jobs in their city, and everything seemed like it was going fine.

Tyson began to notice that Janet was unhappy most of the time. He couldn't figure out the source of her sadness.

What Tyson didn't realize is that Janet brought some baggage with her to the marriage. She was stuck in a soul tie relationship with her ex.

Now, please listen to me, everyone comes into a marriage or relationship with a piece of baggage or two or three. It doesn't matter how holy of a Christian you are; if you look carefully, you can identify a piece of baggage you need to get rid of.

One of the reasons new relationships fail is that we're still stuck in the old ones and don't even know it. Soul ties are invisible bonds that wreak havoc in so many relationships and marriages.

In our counseling office, we regularly identify soul ties as a reason many relationships suffer and some fail.

God wants you healthy in your heart and soul. A healthy you will bring forth a healthy relationship. Also, you'll have to be healthy so you can nurse someone else to health.

Marital statistics say that money, poor communication, and sex are the three biggest reasons why marriages end up in divorce. I'd like to present another theory, and that theory is unsolved personal issues or baggage.

Personal issues cause more divorces than money, poor communication, and sex could ever do combined! The root of all relationship issues and problems are unresolved issues, otherwise called a baggage. **The root will always determine the fruit.**

Your baggage might not be that of a soul tie; it might be other personal issues or even generational issues that you are still dealing with.

Let's take the money issue, for example. If someone had a bad spending habit while they were single, what do you think would happen to that habit when they married?

They bring that same money issue into the marriage. This is one of the reasons why I am a very strong proponent of premarital counseling. It exposes the baggage and weakness in you so they can get fixed or healed prior to saying "I do" at the altar.

Initially, one spouse would say that the other is so bad with finances it's jeopardizing their well-being, but upon further inspection, there's a root problem that the spouse is refusing to deal with. That refusal to deal with the root issue causes the fruit of bad money habits to manifest.

The unresolved root issue is the baggage that needs to be unpacked and sorted through in order for the money issue to be resolved.

Marriage is a magnifier. Whatever you don't like about yourself or have an issue working through will eventually come to light. The problem is that after you get married, you now have someone who is with you 24 hours a day, who can see your faults and weaknesses as clear as day. After a while, they will begin to express their grievances with it. The question is, will you be mature enough to work on them or, if possible, resolve them? Personal improvement requires the precious gifts of patience and forgiveness.

Scripture Meditation: "And it shall come to pass in that day, that his burden shall be taken away from off thy shoulder, and his yoke from off thy neck, and the yoke shall be destroyed because of the anointing" (Isaiah 10:27, KJV).

23

Don't Marry A Guy Who Doesn't Turn You On

It's a miserable feeling to be in a relationship with or married to someone you're no longer attracted to. This problem could have been solved from the very beginning if both parties had taken the time to see if they were madly attracted to each other or not.

Statistics show that one of the top three reasons why marriages and relationships fail is the lack of sexual chemistry, which then leads to sexual frustration and then to little or no sex in the bedroom.

If you don't feel chemistry with him on the first and second date, please don't go for the third one. If the chemistry is there, and it's right, you will know and feel it. **When there's no physical**

attraction, there can be no future with you both!

Please do not be deceived; physical attraction is essential to love, sex, and prophetic marriage. This creates happiness in your relationship.

This rule is so important because I have counseled so many single ladies who dated and married even though they didn't have strong physical attraction or chemistry with each other, and it was just a mess.

Some of them I was able to help restore their marriage by teaching them how to be connected and attracted to each other again. I'll be the first to admit that it's so hard to teach chemistry to grown-up folks.

God has put special DNA, hormones, and personality in you that is very attractive to someone out there and will complete you and them together in a near perfect union.

Do not settle and rush into dating someone you have no chemistry with just because they got some money, swag, or some other characteristics that are appealing to you. Trust me, with time, all of those things will wear off, and if there is no strong chemistry, the hole in the union will be revealed.

Chemistry is beyond sexual appeal. There is physical chemistry, mental chemistry, relational chemistry, spiritual chemistry, amongst others.

Sometimes chemistry can be instantaneous or grow over time. When Adam saw Eve, he shouted aloud, "This is the bone of my bone and the flesh of my flesh." The chemistry was instant. Abraham, who is called the father of faith, acknowledged in the scripture below that his wife was beautiful. The one that's most beautiful in your eyes is the one you have the most chemistry with.

The one you can't stop thinking about. His presence is so magnetic, and you don't want it to end.

You want to be married to a wonderful guy who loves you and turns you on mentally, physically, and sexually.

Chemistry is a deep spiritual and physical feeling and attraction you have for someone that you don't necessarily feel for another person. Strong chemistry means you enjoy the presence of the one you're dating and will not find that same pleasure with another.

If you are already bored just looking at him, please run for your life. Date the one that you see the chemistry still at a high intensity 30 years from now.

Let me be brash with you: Do not date someone you won't like to see naked. Ladies, please don't date a guy that does not stimulate your mind and make your world melt when he puts his hand on your shoulders. Of course just because you have strong chemistry for someone doesn't mean they are the right man or woman for you.

Scripture Meditation: "And Adam said: "This is now bone of my bones And flesh of my flesh; She shall be called Woman, Because she was taken out of Man" (Genesis 2:23, KJV).

24

Build Your Financial Independence

Dear Single Lady, you don't need a guy to come rescue you from financial hardship and difficulties. You can make your own money and be rich even before he finds you. A queen never waits for a king to come rescue her. A queen brings so much to the table. She manages her life and money so well that he cannot resist her offer and partnership.

A king wants a promise for a wife and not a project.

Bad spending habits can ruin a loving relationship faster than anything you think. Now, here is the catch: to be truly financially healthy, **you have to first be healthy in your soul.** *How you handle money shows something about your emotional health.* A bad spender has a broken soul. If you are an impulsive spender, it could mean that you are trying to use the purchase of new things to hide or mask a pain, trauma, hurt, or abuse in your life. More money can never take the pain away, and new things cannot substitute for the need for healing and/or deliverance in your life.

Also, if you and your potential partner are selfish with money, then I can guarantee that you both will be selfish in affection as well. *A financially selfish and stingy person is a person that will be selfish with their love and emotions.*

I will say it another way: a person that is selfish with money will also be selfish with their love and will withhold their feelings and emotions from you.

You need to understand how you look at and deal with money individually and together as a team. Knowing this information now will save you lots of problems in your marriage. Another mistake many couples make about money is spending more money on their wedding than they can afford. They plan financially for their wedding but not their marriage. And then months and years into the marriage, they are still busy paying off debts and the credit cards they spent to impress people on their wedding day.

Women can often have a tougher time than men when it comes to money and building financial wealth. That's not because women are bigger spenders than men or that they simply aren't interested in building wealth and investing. The truth is, there are real structural roadblocks to attaining financial freedom for women compared to their male counterparts. As you already know, I am a serious advocate for financial independence for women.

Start a business or invest in a business.

Here are some tips that can help you towards financial independence and wealth building:

1. Life Coaching – Get Certification at www.naacctraining.com
2. Christian Counseling - Get Certification at www.naacctraining.com
3. Rent out your vehicles – Hyrecar.com and Turo.com
4. Tax preparation
5. Freelance photography services
6. Consulting services
7. Personal fitness trainer
8. Website designer
9. Graphics and printing services

10. Online training
11. Start a business networking group
12. Realtor services
13. Singing/voiceover services
14. Administrative services
15. Cleaning
16. Cooking/catering
17. Ghostwriting and editing
18. Drive for Uber/Lyft
19. Marketing/public relations
20. T-shirt business
21. Wedding consultant/services
22. Credit repair services – www.creditzilla.org

Scripture Meditation: "A feast is made for laughter, and wine maketh merry: but money answereth all things" (Ecclesiastes 10:19, KJV).

25

Relationships Shouldn't Be Just About Sex

You probably couldn't wait to hear my thoughts on the subject of sex. Let me start by saying that sex is beautiful within the confines of marriage. It's one of God's best gifts to mankind.

Sexual attraction is very important in dating; and if you're dating someone with whom you have no sexual attraction, the relationship doesn't stand a chance.

Yet if the relationship is built on sex alone, you'll be in trouble after the second time of sex. Soon enough, the real pressures and trials of your relationship will begin to test your relationship such as dealing with personality differences, attitudes, money worries, career problems, aging, in-laws, and everything else.

Dear Single Lady, it is so important to remember that you are looking for love and not just mere sex. If you disobey this rule, the danger is that you will mistake lust for love. You will think that because the sex is great, the feeling of utopia will last forever. **Please don't go into a relationship because you are sex starved.** That is absolutely the worst reason to get into the dating game.

A relationship that is mostly physical and sexual in nature is built on the wrong foundation. Why do you really want to be in a relationship with him? I hope the answer is because you love him, and he makes you feel better about yourself. Sometimes people will fake that they love you just so that they can have access into your private parts and defile you.

The fact is that most guys will tell on themselves on the very first date. They will reveal their true motive in wanting to date you. Sometimes the clues they give might be so subtle that if you're not paying attention, you might miss them. If they want to go to your house after the first date, their motive is probably wrong. **True love can wait, but lust and infatuation is never patient.**

Scripture Meditation: "If the foundations be destroyed, what can the righteous do?" (Psalm 11:3, KJV).

26

It is very dangerous to marry a narcissistic, self-centered and stingy man. Run!

A man who is selfish with his money will also be selfish with love, care and in the bedroom. You deserve a partner that cares the world about you and is not afraid to show it.

God's plan is for you to date and be in matrimony with someone that cares so much about you, your joy, your happiness, your likes and dislikes, hopes, dreams, and fears. This person will fight a tiger with their bare hands if they perceive you're in danger.

They will take off their coat for you in the rain and give you their lunch if that was all they had. You want a partner who makes you feel special because you are, and they want you to know it.

The truth is that if your partner really cares about you, they will make it very clear, not just in words but also in deeds.

Ask yourself this simple question: Does he care about my feelings, emotions, fears, and wellbeing? Will he go out of his way to make me feel happy even if it comes at a personal discomfort to him?
Don't date or marry a self-centered guy who is incapable of caring for you.

Some people are great at being lovers, and sadly, some just aren't. We see in relationships that once certain people have known you through all seasons, they become complacent and take you for granted. They haven't got time for your problems, neither will they go out of their way to make you happy. They don't bring you flowers anymore, take you out on romantic evenings or spoil you on your birthday. This book is about finding love and happiness in your life and relationship.

A man that doesn't show he cares before marriage will only get worse. Sadly, this kind of person isn't likely to change, at least not for you.

Date someone who really wants to make you happy because they care about you deeply. Date someone who really wants you. If he doesn't care about you now, it will only get worse. Don't imagine that moving in together or saying "I do" is going to make things get better and change him. Don't miss the one that will truly care for you for the one that doesn't.

A self-centered man only cares about himself and can never truly love you like you deserve. Most people enter into a dating relationship by way of the 'in love' experience. They meet someone, and almost instantly, they feel a strong physical, emotional, and sometimes sexual response in their soul. The bells go off, and now they claim that they are 'in love.'

That warm, tingly feeling seems so real. Yet it is not love but infatuation. It's hard to really be in love with someone you just met—someone you hardly know. True love is built on character and balanced chemistry and not mere feelings. True love is not always exciting. There's a vast difference between love and infatuation. Are you in love, or are you suffering from infatuation?

Sadly, a lot of people miss love because they are looking for the wrong signs in finding love. They are looking for the heart palpitations; warm, tingly feelings; and all the bells and whistles. At its peak, the 'in love' experience is exhilarated. Both parties are emotionally obsessed with each other. They go to bed at night and wake up thinking of each other. The eternity of the 'in love' experience is fiction, not fact.

Eventually, however, we all descend from cloud nine back to planet earth. Our senses, personality, and values get activated after been dormant throughout all this while. We now realize that some of his personality traits are actually irritating. He burst into uncontrollable rage and anger when things don't go his way. Those little traits that we overlooked when we were in love now become a huge issue.

Scripture Meditation: "Love is patient. Love is kind. Love isn't jealous. It doesn't sing its own praises. It isn't arrogant. It isn't rude. It doesn't think about itself. It isn't irritable. It doesn't keep track of wrongs. It isn't happy when injustice is done, but it is happy with the truth. Love never stops being patient, never stops believing, never stops hoping, never gives up" (1 Corinthians 13:4–7).

27

Don't Give Up The Cookie (too soon)

What I am about to say now will shock you. **The reality is that men really lose respect for the woman who gives up sex too soon.**

Yet there are plenty of guys out there that will pretend and do all the right things just to eventually seduce you into sex and then dump you.

Sex may dominate our thoughts, dreams, and late night fantasies, but the reality is that the suspense of when it will finally happen when we're in a new relationship is more exciting than the act itself.

You should wait to have sex because you want more than a hookup or fling. You should also wait for sex because God said so, and He knows what is best for you. *You know you deserve more than a one-night stand.*

A young lady told me the last guy she really liked wanted her to go home with him after their first meeting. She said, "Not tonight," and she never heard from him again. Clearly, he was just interested in sex, and she was glad she found that out before things went further.

Listen to this, I have had many men confide in me over the years that when they got serious about marriage, *they didn't consider the girl they had plenty of sex with*. They wanted a new mountain they haven't conquered. **The entry of premature sex complicates things in a relationship.**

The easiest way to make a potential mate to lose interest in you is to give up the **'cookie'** too soon.

If you sleep with a guy too soon, you completely remove the mystique. Even the nicest guy will lose interest if you sleep with him quickly. If you give him access to everything right off the bat, there is nothing to work toward or look forward to. Engage him with your mind. Make him want more time with you.

Nowadays, there seems to be no spiritual or moral standards when it comes to sexual relations. People just have sex indiscriminately, pass diseases and form unhealthy soul ties and carry all those bondages from one relationship to another.

Back in the day, mothers taught their daughters to make him work for 'it.' Even Steve Harvey says women should wait 90 days before sexual contact with a suitor.

God knows it best because He knows and created all things.

For Guys: The strongest way you can show her that you love and care for her is to wait for marriage to have sex with her. Especially if you think she might have potential to be your girlfriend or future wife, you don't want to jump into bed with her too soon because she might question your motives and wonder if you're a player and do the same with other women.

Another reason to wait for sex is that waiting promotes good communication in dating. When a couple practices abstinence, their communication is good because they are not just focused on pleasure but on the joy of sharing their views and experiences; moreover, their conversations are deeper. By contrast, physical intimacy is an easy way to relate, but it overshadows other forms of communication. It is a way of avoiding the real work involved in emotional intimacy, like talking about deep personal issues and working on the basic differences between the two of you.

When a guy just wants to lie with you, it shows he is not really interested in getting to know you!

Waiting for sex encourages contribution instead of selfishness.

Sexual relations in dating can lead to selfishness and a focus on self-satisfaction. They can lead people to feel like they are competing with others with whom their partner may find more attractive. It fosters insecurity and selfishness because when you get sexually intimate, the tendency is to ask for more and more.

Sex before marriage often leads to divorce.

Couples who wait are more likely to succeed in marriage. Research has shown that couples who were sexually active and cohabited are likely to divorce than those who have not cohabited and waited on sex.

You are too valuable to just give in to cheap sex.

Take the time to develop a substantial understanding of the potential partner. Take time to pray together, attend church together, read the Bible together and develop a meaningful and substantive platform for the future.

Dating is a crucial stage in any relationship. It means that the both of you have matriculated from the friendship level, are now exclusive and courting for marriage. Dating is actually a courting and preparation phase for marriage.

Please allow me to say again that the dating stage of the relationship is not merely the 'checking out each other' phase. Checking each other out is what you do in the friendship stage. Don't date senselessly and don't settle. You're God's child, and you deserve someone special just like you.

Build a deeper level of commitment in your relationship before sex is involved. In God's perspective, the best and righteous way to enjoy sex is in the context of marriage. Statistics show that couples who wait for marriage to be sexually involved enjoy a more meaningful sexual intimacy.

Sex is more meaningful to a woman if she feels loved and secure in the relationship. Sex is one of the best ways a wife can affirm her husband and make him feel wanted and loved.

Sexual intimacy is necessary for a healthy relationship. A man needs sex. Women need sex too. Men often want sex more than women do. God made him like that. No medicine or drug can relieve and relax a man like good sex with the woman he loves.

Sex is a very vital part of any healthy relationship.
Don't marry someone who doesn't turn you on.
But Dear Single Ladies, don't give up the cookie (too soon).

Scripture Meditation: "Now as to the matters of which you wrote: It is good (beneficial, advantageous) for a man not to touch a woman [outside marriage]" (1 Corinthians 7:1, AMP).

31 Ways To Know He's Not Into You

1. You make up stories in your head that are different from what you are seeing with your eyes
2. He doesn't compliment you
3. He doesn't mirror your body language
4. You can't remember the last time he did something nice for you
5. He lacks eye contact when you guys are talking
6. When you're on the phone, he doesn't pay much attention to the conversation or you

7. He compares you to others

8. He doesn't return your calls

9. You always hear excuses as to why he didn't return your call(s)

10. He only texts and doesn't desire to hear your voice

11. He avoids meeting your friends

12. He doesn't show interest in the things you're interested in

13. He becomes increasingly short with you

14. He talks about trivial things instead of things of substance (even if you disagree, being able to have the conversation is important)

15. His behavior with others is more warm and friendly than his behavior with you

16. He doesn't touch you or rub you

17. He doesn't do things that make you feel positive or sexy

18. You are the one always asking questions and contributing to the conversation

19. Everyone else's plans are important, except the plans you guys make together

20. He doesn't like spending money on you

21. He doesn't like spending time with you

22. He dresses in ways he knows will not impress you or get your attention towards him

23. He doesn't support you and your endeavors

24. You feel like he acts more annoyed than happy to be with you

25. He doesn't want to be seen with you

26. You guys don't have pet names for each other (honey, sweetie, sugar, etc.)

27. He always asks you to do for him, but when you ask him to do for you, it's a problem

28. He doesn't express interest or like your social media posts or engagements

29. He doesn't talk about or express what it would be like if you guys have a future together

30. They are not spending their money on you

31. The friendship never transitions into something deeper or meaningful

29

Demolishing Spiritual Forces Of Marital Delays

Could it be that the reason why you are not married yet is that your marriage has been spiritually delayed?

Abigail was single for over twenty years. She went through a bitter and nasty divorce twenty years ago and has been single ever since. She claims she has had a few dates here and there, got engaged once, but other than that, nobody is pursuing her, and she never walked down the altar again. She is frustrated and getting tired of hearing that she needs to wait on God for a mate.

After twenty years, she was done hearing that God was preparing the perfect gentleman for her.

She booked a prophetic one-on-one session with me. Within the first five minutes of our conversation, I could already tell that her marriage was being delayed spiritually by demonic forces and word curses that were placed on her by her ex-husband.

I embarked on a rigorous spiritual exercise of fasting, prayer, coaching, and breaking of curses and demonic spirits.

Three short months after the demolishing of the spiritual forces of marital delays in her life, she met a wonderful Christian gentleman. Within weeks, he proposed to her, and a month after the proposal, they got married.

Deliverance Prayers

Dear Single Lady, open your mouth and confess these prayers over you for the next 30 days:

I bind Satanic harassment and rebuke satanic concentration.

Lord bring to a halt and prohibit all satanic surveillance, all satanic plans, all satanic monitoring and spirits that seek to hinder my life's progress and hold up my marriage.

I bind it now and drown it in the blood of Jesus Christ.
I loose my angels to release my God ordained husband to me now in Jesus name.

I decree and declare that by the anointing of God and the blood of Jesus Christ; covenant contracts, chains, fetters, bondage, proclivities and captivity that are contrary to oppose or hinder the fulfillment of God's original plan and purpose for my life are broken and destroyed.

I am liberated from generational curses, satanic and demonic allegiances & alliances, soul ties, spirits of inheritance and any other curse unknown to me but known by God. Lord sever them by the sword of the Lord, the blood & by the Spirit. I speak to my DNA and declare that I am free from any and all influences passed down from one generation to another biologically, socially, emotionally, physiologically, psychologically, spiritually or by any other channel unknown to me but known to God.

Any plans made unknown to me but known by God to keep me from my Godly married life catch fire in Jesus name.

Lord Let every curse be broken and destroyed. Let every fruit that has been formed due to ungoldly roots be destroyed. Let every ungodly thing that has flourished in my life and into my marriage and other meaningful relationships die like the fig tree Jesus spoke to in the scripture.

I command the root of curses to come out and be purged. I command the fruit to be consumed by fire and come out now. I command every spirit of deception, fear, rejection, perversion, bitterness, unforgiveness, anger to come out now. I command the effects of satanic and demonic plans, strategies and tactics against me and my life purpose to come out now. Loose me now.

Lord cancel every entrance of the demonic in my life. I resist every spirit that acts as a gatekeeper or a doorkeeper to my soul into my life. I renounce any further conscious or unconscious alliance, allegiance, association or covenant. I open myself to divine deliverance by Father God. Father have your way now! Perfect those things concerning me in Jesus name. Perfect those things pertaining to my future in Jesus name. Perfect those things pertaining to my marriage in Jesus name.

I decree and declare that a prayer shield by the anointing and my divine bloodline form hedge of protection around me and hide me from the scourge of the enemy, familiar spirits and any and all demonic personalities making it impossible for them to track me or trace me in the spirit. I am free and moving forward in my God-given purpose and destiny no longer hindered in Jesus name amen.

Confessions and declarations for marriage

Dear Single Lady, confess and declare your marriage until it manifests:

Dear heavenly father, I boldly declare that my marriage and wedding is taking place this year. I see a beautiful wedding ring on my finger and I confess that there is no more delay in my life concerning my marriage.

I totally cut off all fake and counterfeits in my life and I decree that my true husband will find, meet and marry me this year without delay!

I decree right now that I am happily married to the man of my dreams in Jesus mighty name, Amen!

Scripture Meditation: "The weapons we fight with are not the weapons of the world. On the contrary, they have divine power to demolish strongholds" (2 Corinthians 10:4, NIV).

30 Prayers To Manifest Your Spouse

Every year you continue to carry baggage from your past is another year in which the blessings of God are hindered from flowing in your life.

Take these prayers and expound them. Pray them and re-pray them over and over again until God reveals Himself to you in them and develops you in the areas of prayer that you need most.
Be ready for the transformation God will do within you!

Prayers for Wisdom will help you navigate the 'dating scene' and maximize it. Wisdom also gives you direction and focus.

Father, I thank You for the ability to ask for wisdom, and You give it to me liberally. Today, I receive the heavenly wisdom from above to be able to discern the different options of spouses presented to me in Jesus' name, Amen!

Prayers of Discernment will help to reveal who your spouse is and who is not so you don't have to waste your time dating or marrying the wrong person.

Lord, give me eyes to see and ears to hear what Your Spirit is saying to me concerning my spouse. Help me to see the heart instead of the outside and cultivate a love that surpasses understanding.

Prayers of Self-Control will help you to keep yourself pure and holy as a single person in preparation for marriage.

Lord, thank You for supernatural strength on high that allows me to take control over my flesh. I declare that my body is presented to You as a living sacrifice and temple of the Spirit of God. I remain steadfast in my faith and walk in holiness in my body, my mind, and my soul. In Jesus' name, Amen.

Prayers of Value unveil to you the deep treasures that God has deposited within you.

Lord, I bless You, for I am fearfully and wonderfully made. I am a person of value and worthy of marriage. I break any strongholds or mindsets that I have adopted that would convince me otherwise. My day of marriage is coming together and soon in the divine timing of God. In Jesus' name, Amen.

Prayers of Gratitude will open your heart to the blessings and favors of God.

Lord, I thank You in advance, for my marriage and spouse is manifesting now. My desire is to be at peace with myself and my situation as You are working all things together for my good and for my benefit. Every distraction, doubt, fear, and worry are cast away and put behind me.

Prayers of Warfare & Deliverance break every negative spirit and demonic powers trying to delay or prevent your marriage from happening.

I declare that I am moving past the hurts of the past and the limitations I placed on myself. I forget what is behind me and press forward to what is ahead of me.

Trauma, negative experiences, loss, and pains of my past will not be carried into my future. I am free from the weights and baggage that have held me down now in Jesus' name, Amen.

Prayers of healing & Deliverance are necessary for everyone because everyone has been through something that has affected them. Yet when you pray those prayers, you open yourself up to be purified in order for those blockages to be broken and your spouse to come through.

I command my soul to be healed. Every ungodly soul tie, every ungodly emotional, mental and psychological attachments are hereby broken now in the name of Jesus. My spirit is open and receptive to the good things that God has for me.

Scripture Meditation: "That is what the Scriptures mean when God told him, 'I have made you the father of many nations.' This happened because Abraham believed in the God who brings the dead back to life and who creates new things out of nothing" (Romans 4:17, NLT).

31

The Two Reasons Why You Are Still Single

If you've been following my teachings and ministry for a while, you'll always hear me say this iconic phrase: ***You're single for a REASON or for a SEASON!***

Those are only two reasons why you're still single. This statement has helped thousands of women find the reason they were still single; they used the new information to confront the reason and then got married.

Don't just automatically assume that God is the reason why you're single. There are a number of **REASONS** why you are still single:

- Spirit husbands
- Soul ties

- God's timing
- Marital delay
- Generational curses
- Personal issues (fear, trust)
- Psychological damage from the past
- Marriage unpreparedness
- Bad relationship choices
- Unhealthy self-image

Those points listed above are some of the most common reasons why women are single.

To win over the reason or reasons why you are still single, you'll need to first allow God to open your spiritual eyes so you could see what is holding you back and then tackle each one of them to submission.

Also, you may be single for a **SEASON:**
This means you just wait it out and allow God to manifest your prophetic marriage in due time and season. **The danger about this postulation is that most single ladies don't know the difference between a God delay and a demonic delay.**

Here is my personal opinion on this matter: If you have been single for over five years and can't seem to find or be in any meaningful relationship, that is probably a demonic delay. God doesn't need to delay your marriage that long. He is a very loving Father, and He wants to give you the desires of your heart, including a desire to be married. God dictates times and seasons for everything—a time to be born, a time to talk, a time to marry, and even a time to die. Nevertheless, the devil and other factors can play a role in sabotaging, obstructing, or delaying God's times and seasons in our lives. It is also good to know that you have a huge part to play in whatever times and seasons that you are in.

In the Bible, Daniel fasted and prayed, and his answer was released the very day he started fasting and praying, but the Prince of Persia fought, delayed and withstood it for 21 days. Daniel had to have help from Archangel Michael so he could get the answer to his prayers. So, it is possible that your prophetic husband and marriage has already been released by God, and the devil or some other spiritual forces have been working against it to delay and sabotage it.

So now you must arise and stop waiting on God to send or release your husband while God is waiting on you to bind this negative spirit working against your marriage.

You may also be able to delay your marital season due to your own personal issues such as spiritual laziness, disobedience, or unpreparedness towards marriage.

Likewise, you can speed up your marital season for marriage by waging a prophetic prayer of warfare, getting yourself ready, doing the things I told you in this book to do and also by sowing a seed in faith for the release of your spouse.

There are several single ladies I know that sowed a prophetic seed into my ministry in faith for the release of their prophetic marriage, and they all got married in an astonishingly short time.

Scripture Meditation: "But for twenty-one days the spirit prince of the kingdom of Persia blocked my way. Then Michael, one of the archangels, came to help me, and I left him there with the spirit prince of the kingdom of Persia" (Daniel 10:13, NLT).

Bonus Chapter

ESTABLISHING GOOD CREDIT

This section of the book is pulled from my bestselling book **Credit Zilla: Hidden Credit Repair Secrets They Don't Want You To Know**

Grab yourself a copy at Amazon or on my website www.UyiAbraham.com

The very first step you need to take when trying to raise your credit score is to find out what your score is and what it means. Legislation called the FACT Act was passed that allows all Americans to get one free copy of their credit report every year. This report lists all of your debts you've had and your payment history on those debts.

It will tell you where you owe money, how much you owe, and how you pay (on time, 30 days late, etc.). All of that information is compiled together and then analyzed. After the analysis, a number is assigned to you as to what your credit fitness level is. Potential creditors then look at your credit score and decide if you are going to be able to pay back the amount of money you are requesting to borrow.

What A Low Credit Score Really Costs You

Your monthly loan and credit card payments can easily be 40% higher with a low score! A higher credit score can save you an enormous amount of money by qualifying you for a lower mortgage interest rate (and by letting you qualify in the first place).

According to Fair Isaac (at the time of this writing), lenders would probably demand a 5.5% percent interest rate on a $300,000, 30-year fixed mortgage for a borrower with a credit score between 500 and 579. That's a $1,700 monthly payment for principal and interest. But a score above 760 would qualify you for about a 3.3 percent rate with a payment of $1,300 a month. That's savings of $500 each month, and more than $100,000 over the life of the loan!

This chart illustrates just how much a low credit score can cost you over the life of a loan:

So you don't have any credit to speak of, but you have big plans for the future. Maybe you're a fresh college graduate or a young person eager to buy your first new car.

If you have never had to use credit before, first of all BRAVO! Of course, it's best to pay cash for the things you need so that you don't have to worry about credit card payments, loan payments, or interest rates.

But if you're young, the chances of you needing credit in the future are very real. Someday you might want to buy a house. Perhaps you'll want to buy a new car.

If you're building your credit score from scratch, you'll likely need to start with a secured credit card. Apply for a secured credit card.

After you've developed a history of using your secured credit card responsibly you can either ask to be moved to an unsecured credit card or apply for a new unsecured credit card and close the secured card. In either case, providing you have met your obligations on the secured card, you'll get your deposit back.

When you're starting fresh with no credit history at all, here are a few ways to get a good start on establishing good credit:

1. Pay your bills on time, especially mortgage or rent payments. Apart from extreme circumstances like bankruptcy or tax liens, nothing has as big of an impact on your credit history as late payments.

2. Establish credit early. Having clean, active charge accounts established many years ago will boost your score. If you are averse to credit, on principle, consider setting up automatic monthly payments for, say, utilities and phone on a credit card account and locking the card away where it's not a temptation.

3. Don't max out available credit on credit card accounts. Lenders won't be impressed. Instead, they are much more likely to assume that you have trouble managing your finances. Beyond one or two credit cards, it starts to get complicated.

4. Don't apply for too much credit in a short amount of time. Multiple requests for your credit history (not including requests by you to check your file) will reduce your score. If you are hunting around for good loan rates, assume that every time you give your Social Security number to a lender or credit card company, they will order a credit history.

5. Be neat and consistent when filling out credit applications. This will insure that all your good deeds get recorded in a single file, as opposed to multiple files or, worse, someone else's file. Watch out for inconsistencies in use of "Jr." and "Sr."

6. Check your credit history for errors, especially if you will soon be requesting a time-dependent loan, like a mortgage.

One great way to start establishing credit is to apply for a store credit card (Sears, JC Penney, etc.). Once you get the card, make a few small purchases and pay them off completely.

Do this a few times over the course of a year and you'll find yourself with some established credit with an excellent payment history. DO NOT go overboard and buy more than what you can pay for, though.

So let's do a quick review on how to establish a good credit history:

- Apply for a store or gas credit card and make a few charges.
- Ask a loved one to co-sign on a loan.
- Find a respected secured credit card company.
- Open a checking account.
- Don't apply for too many credit cards in too short of a time.
- Check your credit report for any errors.
- Go slowly.
- Don't overspend.
- Make sure your lender reports to at least one of the credit reporting agencies.
- MAKE YOUR PAYMENTS ON TIME!!!!!!!

HOW TO LEGALLY REMOVE DISPUTES

When you have inaccurate items on your credit report, it's important to dispute them, especially if they're negative items that lower your score.

It's your responsibility and in your best interest to fix your credit history whenever you see a problem, and there are legal steps you can take to resolve most issues.

Sometimes items can show up that don't belong to you, or you'll see charged-off accounts which were paid, or something else shows up that isn't your responsibility.

Duplicate accounts have also been known to appear, or older information improperly deleted from a database. In such cases, one of the first steps is recognizing the negative items and making sure they're inaccurate.

If you're not sure, you can still dispute them. However, if you recognize the nature of the mistake, it will help to gather documentation to prove the validity of your dispute to the reporting agencies. More information about how to repair your credit and filing disputes can be found on **www.creditzilla.org**

Credit bureaus are obligated by law to investigate disputes. The question is how well they do it. According to the law, the credit bureaus are required to investigate your disputes unless they consider them to be "frivolous". If your dispute is valid, they will correct your report, but it could take some persistence on your part. After they receive your letter of dispute, it's their responsibility to look into the matter.

Below are the top dispute reasons that are most used:

#1 - I was not 30, 60, or 90 days late in this payment.

#2 - This account does not belong to me.

#3 - This is a duplicate account.

#4 - This account is closed.

#5 - The right credit limit is not being reported.

#6 - This collection was already paid off.

#7 - You are not reporting a positive account on my credit report.

#8 - I never authorized this inquiry.

#9 - This collection/charge-off was paid.

#10 - I never signed a contract.

#11 - This public record has been satisfied/ released/ dismissed/ vacated.

#12 - You are reporting misspelled/ wrong names on my credit report.

#13 - You are reporting the wrong birthdate on my credit report.

#14 - I am an authorized user on this account. Please remove it.

DEAR SINGLE LADY, I Want To Help You Win

Dear Single Lady, it is my highest hope and prayer that this book blessed you, changed your life and also prepared you for your prophetic marriage.

I believe in you, and I believe in your prophetic marriage, and I know that by my prayer for you and you also adhering to and implanting the wisdom in this book, very soon you will be walking down the altar and getting married.

Give me the opportunity and honor to continue to speak into your life, coach and mentor you into your purpose and prophetic marriage.

Become a part of Dear Single Lady Coaching

Sign up for our newsletter and various coaching programs and conferences. We look forward to talking to you soon.

Join Now

www.DearSingleLady.com

Sign up for our newsletter and various coaching programs and conferences. I look forward to talking to you soon.

Join Now

www.DearSingleLady.com